To Joseph

Originally published by Lion Publishing, plc
Oxford, England

This edition © 1997 Lion Publishing
Illustrations © 1997 Danuta Mayer
Text by Mary Joslin
The author asserts the moral right
to be identified as the author of this work

First published in North America in 1998 by
Loyola Press
3441 North Ashland Avenue
Chicago, Illinois 60657

Printed and bound in Spain by Bookprint

The stories and songs that inform this book about angels can be found
in the Old and New Testaments of the Bible.

Library of Congress Cataloging-in-Publication Data

Joslin, Mary, 1953–
    Do the angels watch close by? / Mary Joslin & Danuta Mayer.
       p.   cm.
    Originally published: Oxford, England : Lion Pub., c1997.
    Summary: Descriptions based on Scripture present angels singing,
rejoicing, dancing with delight, and comforting the fearful.
    ISBN 0-8294-1111-9
    1. Angels--Juvenile literature.   [1. Angels.]   I. Mayer, Danuta.
II. Title.
BT966.2.J67 1998
235'.3--dc21
                                    98-11447
                                      CIP
                                      AC

98 99 00 01 02/10 9 8 7 6 5 4 3 2 1

Do the *Angels* watch close by?

M a r y J o s l i n & D a n u t a M a y e r

 Loyola Press

When the night is dark
and those who love you
are fast asleep,
are you alone with
the glow of the moon
and the raggedy clouds
and the blowing wind—
or do the angels
watch close by?

Sometimes the world seems bleak and empty.

Stories and songs
of long ago
tell of the world's beginning.
In the mysterious time
before time began
the Maker God called the
world into being.
From the deepest dark
arose earth and heaven,
sea and sky,
hill and mountain and plain.

*I*n the highest heavens
the angels sang
of the Maker's great
goodness and love.

*Maybe the heavens
hold greater mysteries
than we imagine.*

O n the world below,
the Maker God commanded
the green and growing things
to unfurl their leaves and open
their bright flowers to the sun.
As the fruit ripened in the long
summer days, the angels
rejoiced at the first harvest.

*No one knows for sure what
an angel might be.*

No one can say what an angel might look like.

On land and
sea, the Maker God called
forth all manner of creatures:
animals of the wild lands,
animals of the farmlands,
bright birds and reptiles
and fish of every kind—
while the angels danced with
delight among them.

W hen the Maker God
filled the world with
people, joyfully the angels
joined in their songs... but the
people seemed unaware.

*It is easy for people to
imagine that angels
look like people.*

From time to time there were rumors of angels... of bright shining messengers bringing news of joy and peace from the Maker God in heaven to a dark and fearful world.

If angels come from highest heaven, perhaps they fly down on glistening wings.

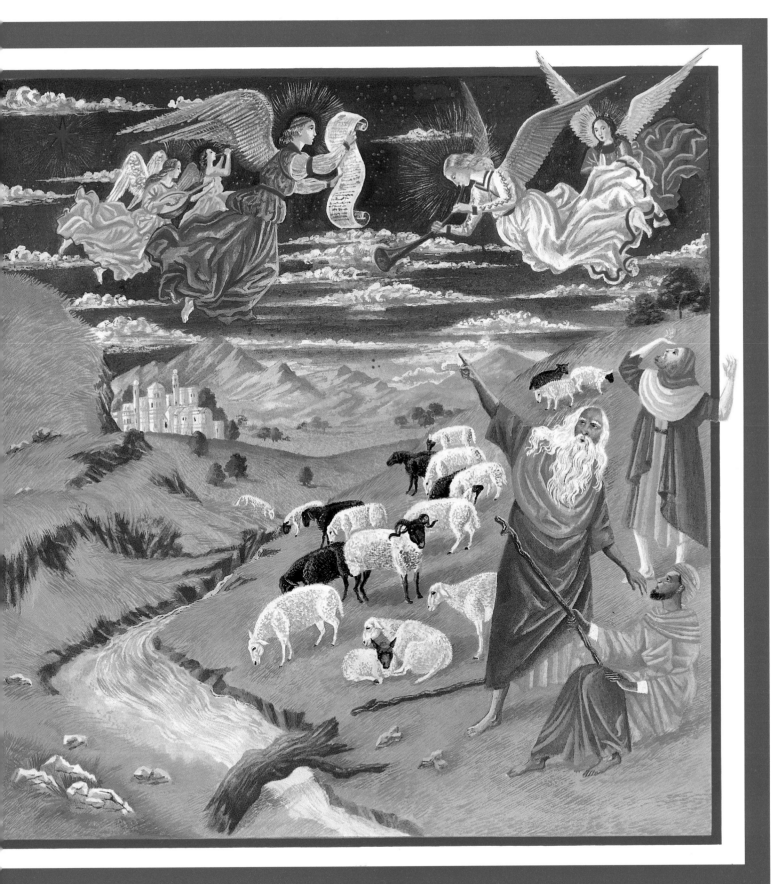

And some, who are thought to be wise, have said that the Maker God has set an angel to guard each and every child.

Can it be true that angels, all unseen, watch with infinite care over all the world?

Imagine angels walking close by, kindly and gentle and strong.

So perhaps, when night's dark shadows fall, angels enfold the fearful in a shimmering embrace.

Imagine angels helping people to find the way ahead.

When the world seems
vast and trackless and
wild, perhaps the
angels show a safe path
to follow.

When the world is good and kind, perhaps the angels in heaven sing together in a joyful celebration.

Imagine the angels dancing among the stars.

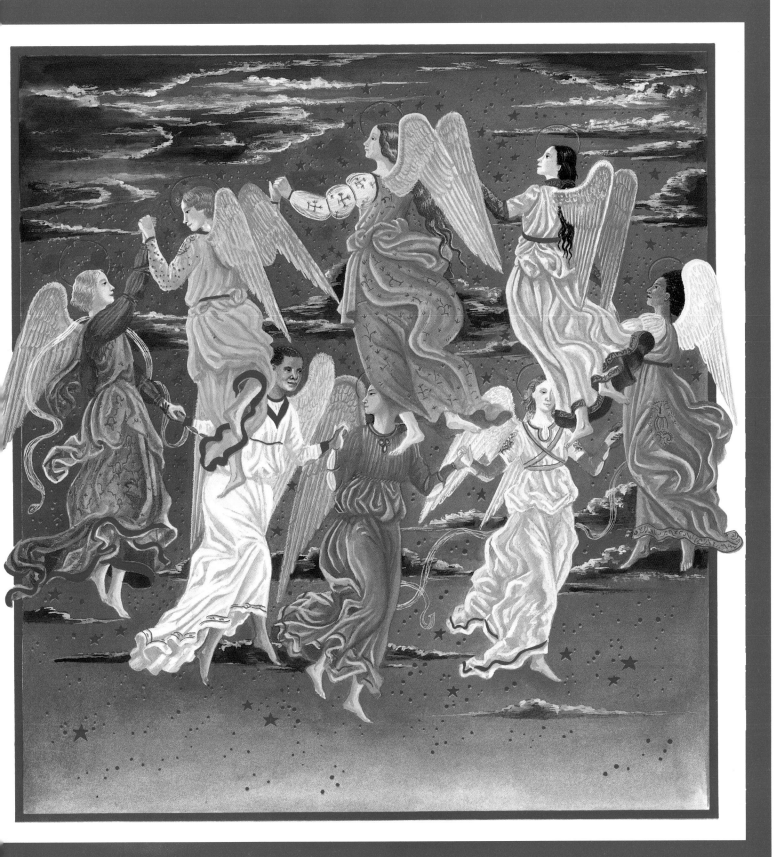

And perhaps one day,
when the world is old
and the Maker God
makes all things new,
people and angels
will live together
in peace and joy and love.

*Some say that
one day, there
will be no need to
imagine angels...
for we will be
with them in a
new heaven, on a
new earth.*